W9-BIU-323

Panayiotis Kalorkoti

A RETROSPECTIVE OF ETCHINGS AND SCREENPRINTS
1978 - 89

 IMPERIAL WAR MUSEUM, LONDON
15 February - 1 April 1990

ISBN 0 901627 56 9

Published by The Imperial War Museum, Lambeth Road, London SE1 6HZ
Copyright © the Trustees of the Imperial War Museum 1990
Catalogue designed by Peter Morrill
Printed by Colden Offset Ltd.

PANAYIOTIS KALORKOTI was almost nine years old when, in 1966, his parents brought him to England from the Northern part of Cyprus. Because he lived in a close Greek Cypriot community he was always acutely aware of the differences between the world into which he was born and that into which he had been moved. His sense of being something of an outsider in England was heightened by his membership of the Greek Orthodox Church whose services he regularly attended until he left school. Not until 1976, when he began to study art at the University of Newcastle, did Kalorkoti begin consciously to distance himself from his background and attempt to come to terms with what he had always regarded (and to an extent continues to regard) as a partly alien culture.

What Kalorkoti describes as his 'slightly schizophrenic' relationship with the traditions and culture of his adopted homeland accounts for both the strengths and weaknesses of his work. On the one hand his familiarity with Greek icon painting has given him insights into the ways visual imagery can convey a multiplicity of meaning and express a wide range of emotion, while, on the other, the speed and eagerness with which he responded to and assimilated a large number of external influences as a student have resulted in a certain inconsistency of style. His artistic development has been marked by a series of interruptions and new beginnings, evident in this exhibition only by the absence of any of the work Kalorkoti produced between 1978 and 1985, years of study first at Newcastle and then, after a break, in the Printmaking Department of the Royal College of Art in London which is where I came to know him.

Even there in that hot-bed of individualism, Kalorkoti seemed somewhat out of place, as much for his grasp of reality and the unusual nature of his ideas as for his rather wild appearance. There was a time when he wandered around the College with two small sketchbooks, asking almost everyone he bumped into to draw a portrait of Kalorkoti in one of the books while he made one of his victim in the other. Almost no-one refused, and the result is a unique and valuable document of the faces of the celebrated and the unknown, from David Hockney to fellow students, who had crossed his path.

Much of the best work of those seven years between 1978 and 1985 consists of portrait etch-ings, not of people Kalorkoti personally knew but of the nineteenth and twentieth century painters he most admired - Whistler, Seurat, Cezanne, Picasso, Matisse, Klee, Pollock and De Kooning. Since these painters are surrounded in the prints by representative examples of their work and by figures and symbols related to their lives, it is as though Kalorkoti was attempting, by purely artistic means, to learn about, to understand his enthusiasm for, and to discover a way of relating to a tradition of which he initially felt himself to have no part. Kalorkoti later turned to quite different subjects, but the compositional and narrative devices he exploited and refined in his tributes to the fathers of modernism reappear in modified form in most of his subsequent work: pictures within pictures, juxtapositions of apparently unrelated imagery which enable him to contrast and compare, to suggest, imply and allude.

The subjects of Kalorkoti's later graphics are, put simply, social and political. They treat not only war and its consequences but also human beings in conflict and distress, and the effects of social conditions on human behaviour. In my view the most memorable of them point to the dangerous attractions of what can only be described as the aesthetics of combat, the seductive glamour of uniforms and the visual appeal of the design of aeroplanes and other weaponry.

The earliest works in this exhibition date from 1978 and they introduce one of the themes dealt with in many of the later prints. They are not etchings, now Kalorkoti's preferred medium, but screenprints, and they present seven transformations of one of the images in Goya's 'Disasters of War' which Kalorkoti first recreated as a small sculpture and then photographed from a variety of angles. The prints made from the photographs are bold and striking, and their appearance, roughened by the obtrusive use of screen dots, is consciously crude. They imitate the look of newspaper photographs in order not only to add drama and urgency, but also to stress the contemporaneity and universality of a message conveyed by an image that was originally inspired by an event which Goya witnessed in the Peninsular War of 1804 - 14.

It was with these Goya variations that Kalorkoti's work achieved something close to a political dimension. He came to believe that art can influence the way people think and act and was consequently drawn to the work of those artists of the past who employed the grotesque and satirical in order to comment on the human condition: Hogarth and Daumier as well as George Grosz and Otto Dix.

Kalorkoti's enthusiasm for such artists explains the affinities between so much of his imagery and cartoons. Yet he is eager to stress that, important though cartoons can be, they remain ephemeral, locked into the time and the circumstances which gave them birth. Hogarth, Goya, Daumier, Grosz and Dix were able to comment on the passing scene in a way which gave it universal validity, a significance which will be preserved for future generations. For Kalorkoti, etching, a medium which evokes many rich associations, is chiefly a way of giving his imagery the kind of permanence appropriate to his message.

Like Grosz, Kalorkoti also uses the technique of photomontage. He juxtaposes found, photographic images in order to imply meaning through conjunction. The two Berlin etchings which he made in 1985 after a brief but plainly memorable visit to the city, are composed of details of photographs, mostly of historic landmarks on both sides of the Wall, arranged rather like a comic strip. But apart from the fragments of graffiti on the wall itself, there are no words, no text and no story, only the ambiguous message that is suggested by dramatic pictures artfully cropped and juxtaposed in a way which makes the familiar scene surprisingly new. The variety and placing of the imagery suggest a multiplicity of shifting connections, relationships and commentaries, and these two prints remain as memorable as they were before the events of November 1989 transformed the face of Eastern Germany.

The technique - in which a collage or photomontage is transformed into a monochrome or coloured etching - is an effective tool for the expression of a complex message or idea by means of suggestion and allusion. It has also enabled Kalorkoti to present a mass of complex information in a visually arresting and quickly comprehensible manner. When, in 1988, he was commissioned by the Imperial War Museum to make two prints in which something of the extraordinary wealth and variety of the Museum's collections would be suggested, he chose to employ photomontage in order to combine details of maps, fragments of text, symbols, portraits and other images, and to give visual coherence and meaning to a mass of confusing information. The use of geometric grids in these coloured etchings, the startling contrasts of scale and viewpoint, of close and wide focus, stimulate the eye to explore the wealth of detail and to establish connections between the various parts.

With the exception of the Goya screenprints, all of Kalorkoti's graphics employ collage or photomontage to some extent. 'Soldier' of 1987 (which was followed two years later by a series of a further eight related images with the same title) is a dramatic transformation of a photograph of a head, made both sinister and comic by the gas mask which both obscures and mimics the features. Three graffiti-like, faux-naif faces at the base of the composition stress the fearful, totemic aspect of the larger image which takes on the character of some ritualistic mask. The later prints with the same title adopt the same compositional device of a minor image which comments on the major 'portrait'. Seen together, these etchings suggest the common humanity of combatants, no matter what uniform they wear or what flag they march under. As important, however, is what they have to say about the power of uniform to dehumanise and alienate while losing nothing of their visual appeal. 'Soldier 8' - based on a famous photograph of a member of the Afrika Corps, his head protected against the sun and sand - is powerful and memorable. With Kalorkoti's background in mind, it is tempting to describe it as an entirely modern icon.

Frank Whitford

1. Homage to Goya No. 1

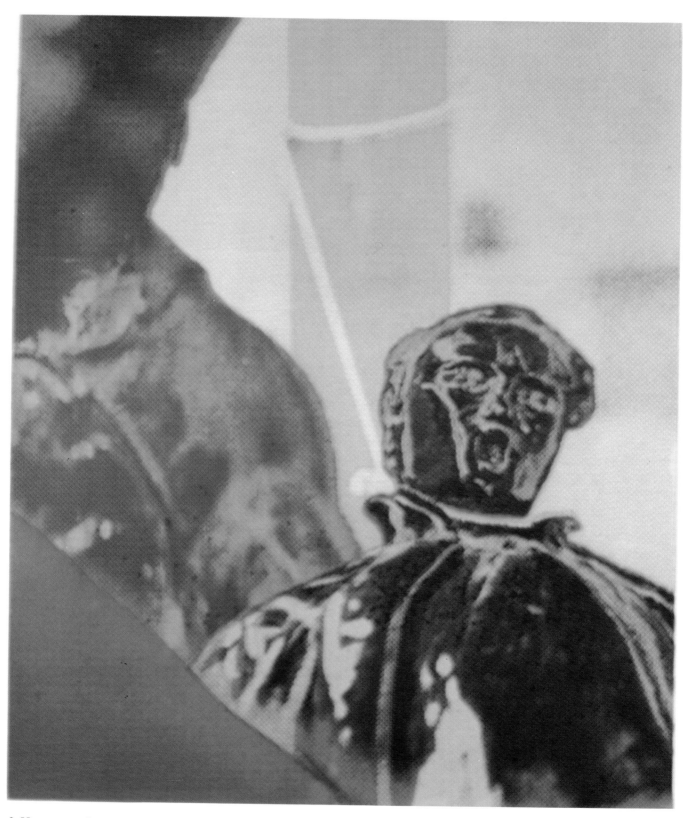

2. Homage to Goya No. 2

3. Homage to Goya No. 3

4. Homage to Goya No. 4

5. Homage to Goya No. 5

6. Homage to Goya No. 6

7. Homage to Goya No. 7

8. Berlin

9. Berlin (East and West)

11. Untitled / Faces

10. *Detail* : Berlin (East and West)

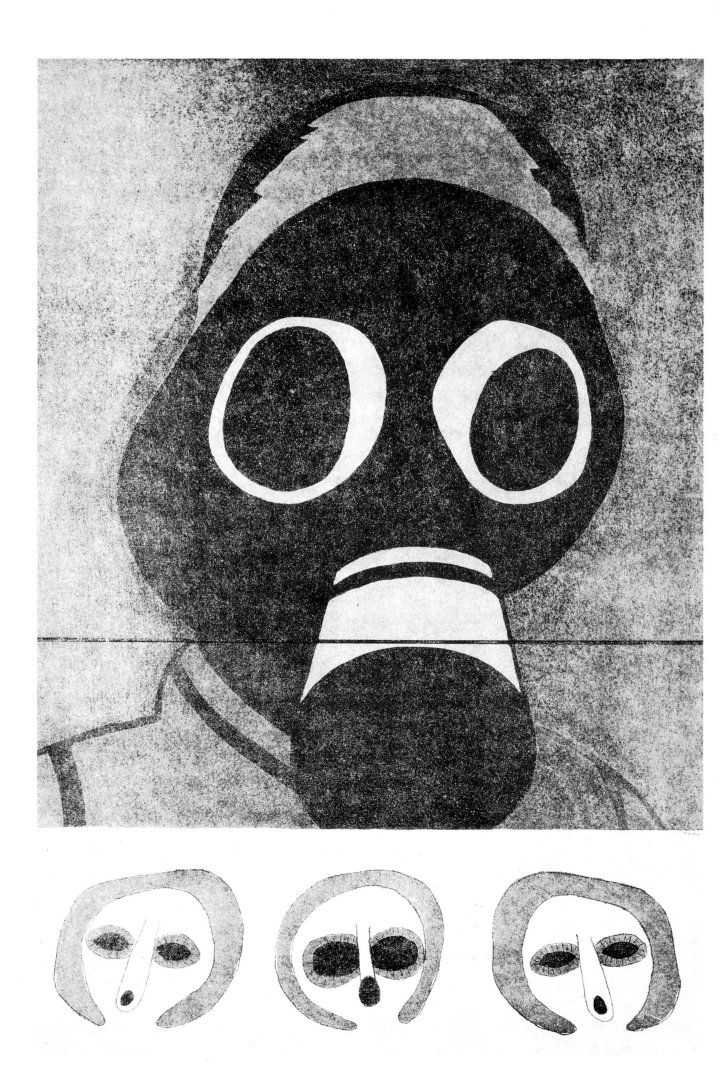

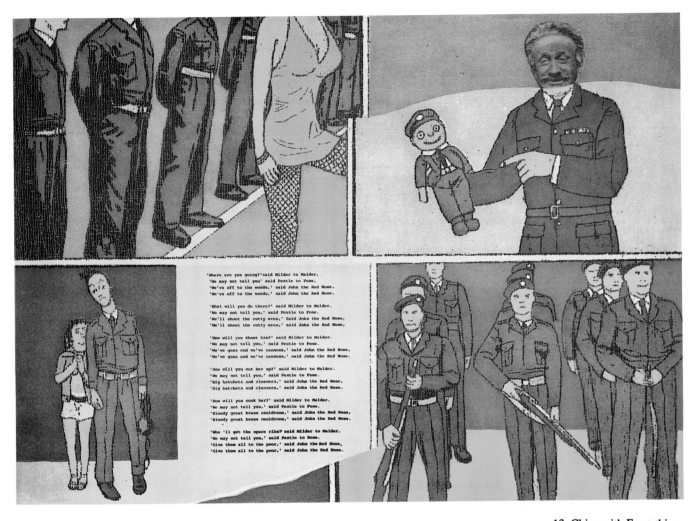

13. Chips with Everything

12. Soldier

14. The Ordered Condition

15. Untitled / Playhouse

16. Untitled / Composition

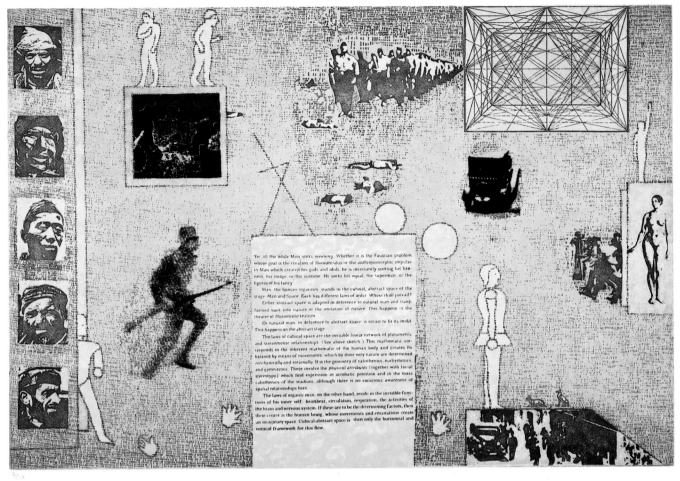

17. Untitled / Order

18. Untitled / Struggle

19. Untitled / Memory

20. Untitled / Reflections

21. *Detail:* Soldier 7

22. Hartlepool Commission No. 1

23. Hartlepool Commission No. 2

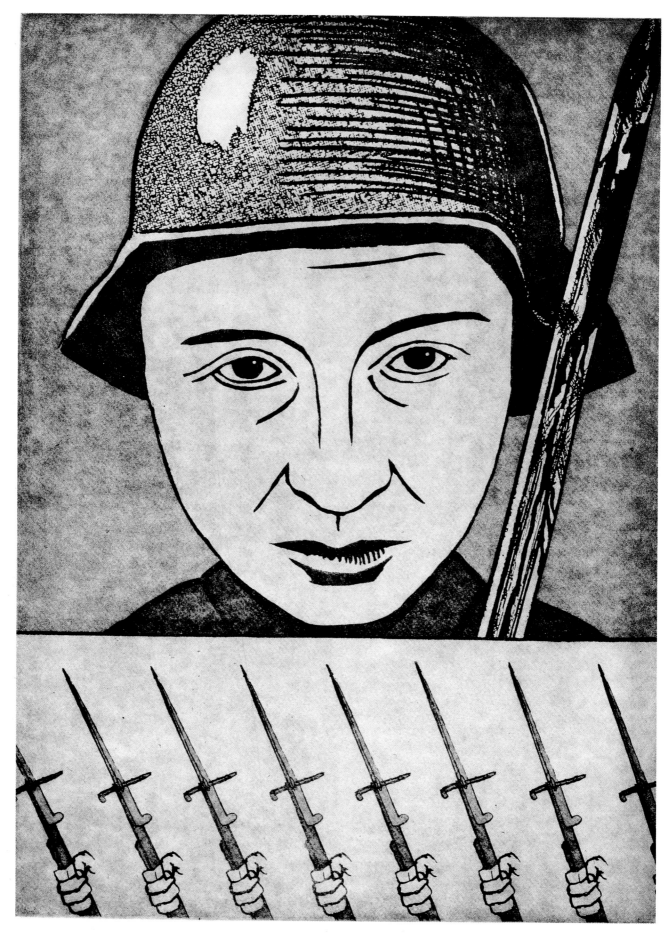

24. Soldier 1

25. Soldier 2

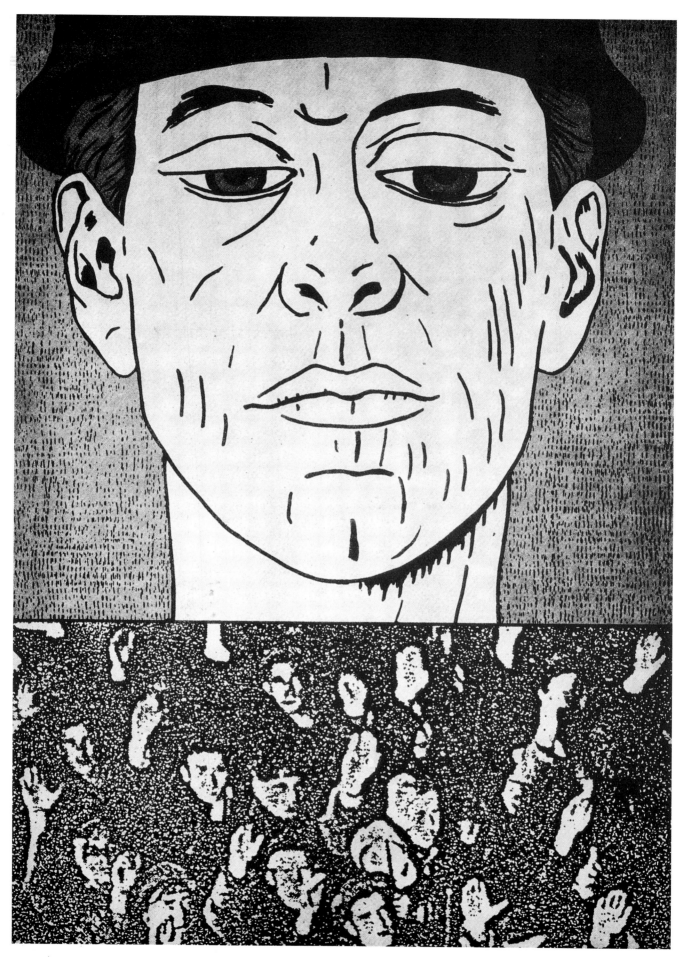

26. Soldier 3

27. Soldier 4

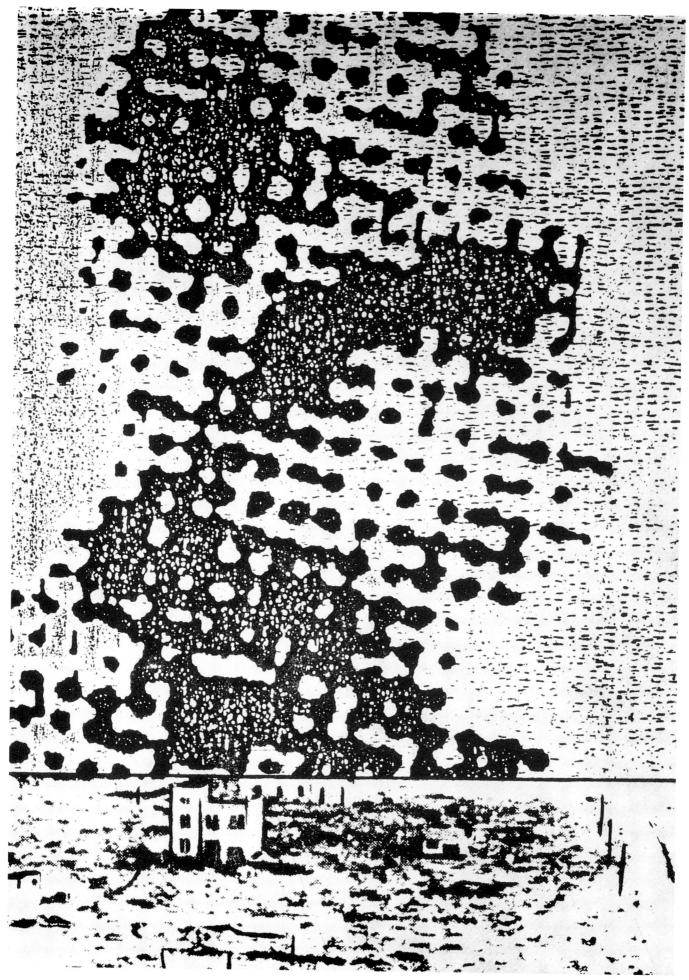

28. Soldier 5

29. Soldier 6

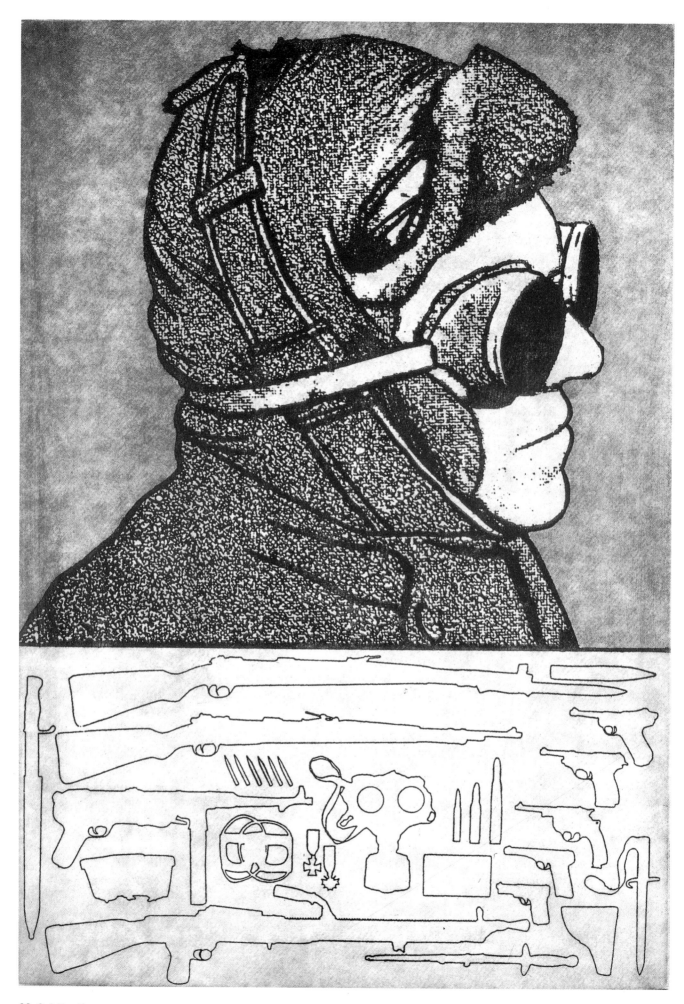

30. Soldier 7

31. Soldier 8

BIOGRAPHY

Born in Cyprus 1957

Studied for his B.A. Hons. in Fine Art at Newcastle upon Tyne University where he was awarded a first class degree in 1980. Went to the Royal College of Art, London, where he studied for and was awarded an M.A. in 1985. Immediately following his degree exhibition, Kalorkoti was appointed Artist in Residence at Leeds Playhouse. During 1986/87 he studied at Koninklijke Akademie voor Kunst en Vormgeving, 's-Hertogenbosch on a Netherlands Government Scholarship and on his return to Britain he became the first Bartlett Fellow in the Visual Arts at Newcastle upon Tyne University in 1988. Subsequently he was commissioned by the Imperial War Museum, People's Theatre, Newcastle, Darlington Arts Centre, Gray Art Gallery and Museum, Hartlepool, Grisedale Society (Theatre in the Forest) and the National Garden Festival (Gateshead).

SOLO EXHIBITIONS

1980   Newcastle Polytechnic Gallery

1981   Bede Gallery, Jarrow

1982   Bede Monastery Museum, Jarrow
        Ceolfrith Gallery, Sunderland Arts Centre
        Pentonville Gallery, London

1984   Abbot Hall Gallery, Kendal

1987   The Minories, Colchester
        Steendrukkerij Amsterdam B.V.

1988-89 Hatton Gallery, Newcastle (Tour: Darlington Arts Centre; Gray Art Gallery and Museum, Hartlepool; Queen's Hall Arts Centre, Hexham)

1990   Imperial War Museum, London

GROUP EXHIBITIONS

1980   The Stone Gallery, Newcastle

1981   'Small Works' Newcastle Polytechnic Gallery

1982   'and Printmaking' Waterloo Gallery, London

1983   'Stowells Trophy' Royal Academy of Arts, London
        'Northern Young Contemporaries' (awarded Granada Prize) Whitworth Art Gallery, Manchester

1984   Bath Festival Painting Competition
        'New Contemporaries' ICA, London

1985   'Printmakers at the Royal College of Art' Concourse Gallery, Barbican Centre
        'Fresh Air' St. Paul's Gallery, Leeds
        'Whitworth Young Contemporaries' Whitworth Art Gallery, Manchester

1986   'Tradition and Innovation in Printmaking Today' Concourse Gallery, Barbican Centre (tour: Milton Keynes Exhibition Gallery; Ferens Art Gallery, Hull; Andrew Grant Gallery, Edinburgh; Aspex Gallery, Portsmouth)
        'Between Identity and Politics, A New Art' Gimpel Fils, London (tour: Darlington Arts Centre; Gimpel and Weitzenhoffer, New York)
        'Fresh Art' Concourse Gallery, Barbican Centre

1987   Athena Art Awards, Concourse Gallery, Barbican Centre
        'Which Side of the Fence' Imperial War Museum, London

1989   'The Artistic Records Committee: A Retrospective 1972-1989' Imperial War Museum, London

1990   National Garden Festival (Gateshead)

CATALOGUE

1. Homage to Goya No. 1 1978
   Screenprint 42 x 59.7 cm
   Edition of 9

2. Homage to Goya No. 2 1978
   Screenprint 59.7 x 42 cm
   Edition of 6

3. Homage to Goya No. 3 1978
   Screenprint 42 x 59.7 cm
   Edition of 5

4. Homage to Goya No. 4 1978
   Screenprint 59.7 x 42 cm
   Edition of 6

5. Homage to Goya No. 5 1978
   Screenprint 42 x 59.7 cm
   Edition of 9

6. Homage to Goya No. 6 1978
   Screenprint 59.7 x 42 cm
   Edition of 5

7. Homage to Goya No.7 1978
   Screenprint 42 x 59.7 cm
   Edition of 11

8. Berlin 1985
   Multi-Plate Etching 56.5 x 75.5 cm
   Edition of 40

9. Berlin (East and West) 1985
   Etching 57.1 x 76.2 cm
   Edition of 40

10. *Detail*: Berlin (East and West)

11. Untitled/Faces 1987
    Etching 50.1 x 62.2 cm
    Edition of 10

12. Soldier 1987
    Etching 62.2 x 50.1 cm
    Edition of 10

13. Chips with Everything 1985
    Multi-Plate Etching 56.5 x 76.2 cm
    Edition of 50

14. The Ordered Condition 1985
    Multi-Plate Etching 56.5 x 76.2 cm
    Edition of 50

15. Untitled/Playhouse 1985
    Multi-Plate Etching 56.5 x 76.2 cm
    Edition of 50

16. Untitled/Composition 1987
    Multi-Plate Etching 56.5 x 76.2 cm
    Edition of 10

17. Untitled/Order 1988
    Multi-Plate Etching 56.5 x 76.2 cm
    Edition of 10

18. Untitled/Struggle 1988
    Multi-Plate Etching 56.5 x 76.2 cm
    Edition of 10

19. Untitled/Memory 1988
    Multi-Plate Etching 56.5 x 76.2 cm
    Edition of 10

20. Untitled/Reflections 1985
    Multi-Plate Etching 61 x 57.1 cm
    Edition of 50

21. *Detail*: Soldier 7

22. Hartlepool Commission No. 1 1989
    Multi-Plate Etching 56.5 x 75.5 cm
    Edition of 10

23. Hartlepool Commission No. 2 1989
    Multi-Plate Etching 56.5 x 75.5 cm
    Edition of 10

24. Soldier 1 1989
    Etching 62.2 x 49.8 cm
    Edition of 10

25. Soldier 2 1989
    Etching 62.2 x 49.8 cm
    Edition of 10

26. Soldier 3 1989
    Etching 62.2 x 49.8 cm
    Edition of 10

27. Soldier 4 1989
    Etching 62.2 x 49.8 cm
    Edition of 10

28. Soldier 5 1989
    Etching 62.2 x 49.8 cm
    Edition of 10

29. Soldier 6 1989
    Etching 62.2 x 49.8 cm
    Edition of 10

30. Soldier 7 1989
    Etching 62.2 x 49.8 cm
    Edition of 10

31. Soldier 8 1989
    Etching 62.2 x 49.8 cm
    Edition of 10

32. Imperial War Museum Commission No.1 1988
    Multi-Plate Etching 56.5 x 76.2 cm
    Edition of 10

33. Imperial War Museum Commission No. 2 1988
    Multi-Plate Etching 56.5 x 76.2 cm
    Edition of 10

32. Imperial War Museum Commission No. 1

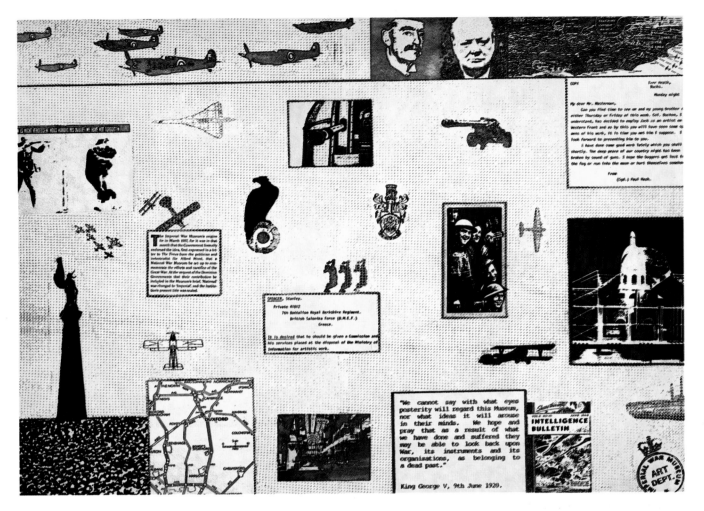

33. Imperial War Museum Commission No. 2

Cover Illustration: Imperial War Museum
Commission No.1. 1988